A NEW LEXICON

ENTRIES FROM A
PERSONAL FIELD GUIDE

Maralee Gerke 2014

A NEW LEXICON
ENTRIES FROM A
PERSONAL FIELD GUIDE

MARALEE GERKE

DANCING MOON PRESS
NEWPORT, OREGON

Paperback ISBN: 978-1-937493-69-1
Library of Congress Control Number: 2014943343
Manufactured in the United States of America

Gerke, Maralee
A New Lexicon: Entries from a Personal Field Guide
1. Poetry
I. TITLE

Cover design & production: Sarah Gayle and Wayne Plourde,
SolaLuna Studios
Book editing, design, & production: *Carla Perry, Dancing Moon Press*

DANCING MOON PRESS
P.O. Box 832, Newport, OR 97365
541-574-7708
www.dancingmoonpress.com
info@dancingmoonpress.com

First Edition

FOR MY HUSBAND, ROBIN
WHO ALWAYS ENCOURAGES ME

Contents

THE TASTE OF ROCKS

THE STING OF THORNS

NATURAL HISTORY

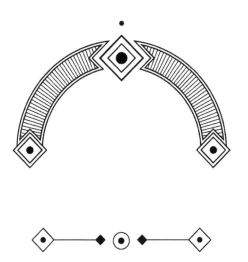

Natural History

"The beginning of wisdom is calling things by their right names."
—Chinese Saying

Once I knew the name of the maples
that drag their heavy leaves along the foggy pane.

Born into the mystery of fir and oak,
of trout lilies and licorice fern,
that world was familiar, ordinary.

Moody, but mutable
I have adapted to more arid climes,
bitterroot, sage, and juniper my new lexicon.

In the unpublished manuscript
of my personal field guide,
new trees, birds, and flowers

measure my immigrant status.

Transplanted into an unfamiliar landscape
I have pared down, become spare
finally the right shape for the desert.

LADY'S SLIPPER AND LAMBS' TONGUES

Scrambling up through the
field of spring beauties, I broke twigs
on the scrub oaks, collected
cockleburs on my pant legs,
and risked poison oak, until
at the edge of the forest I collapsed
at the base of the crippled maple.
One limb flung out near the ground
as broad as our milk cow,
covered with thick chartreuse moss
and lacy licorice root ferns.
Straddling the limb, I
lifted the moss and tore out the root:
a taste of anise, wild and tangy in my mouth.

I was as wild as the flowers, that
grew in profusion amid the grass and moss.
I picked Johnny-jump-ups,
Lambs' Tongues, and the elusive Lady's Slipper.
Back down the hill I ran, hands full of
half-wilted wildflowers.
My proffered nosegay plopped in a canning jar of water on
the windowsill above the kitchen sink.

Looking back, I know I've been separated too long from
the geography of my childhood,
and now I venture beyond the garden fence with
trepidation and longing to be somewhere more tame.

GOLD STARS

Too early for bees,
Gold Stars glisten in
a spreading yellow carpet.
Their golden tongues beckon
me to lie down and
pollinate my dreams.

THE SENTINELS

Two cats crouched in waiting stillness
on my front walk this morning.
Paws folded beneath heavily furred bodies,
they purr their soft breath into the cool air.
From the porch I watch, as they meditate
on ephemeral cat secrets with half-closed eyes.

As one, they rise and stretch, pink tongues
curling slightly at the tip, then saunter
back across the street for a breakfast of tuna.
Stretching left and right I press my palms
to the warm places they've relinquished
and sit alone with the essence of cats
in perfect morning silence.

Refuge

Blanketed in bitterbrush and sage,
sandy hills roll toward the horizon.
A gravel path curves into the juniper forest
around the lee of an ancient mountain.
Creeping phlox show clumps of magenta
and in the shade, yellow bells bloom.

My shadow spreads over the rocky ground
as I walk toward the mingling of water and earth.
Red winged blackbirds cling to thick lines of dried cattails.
Placid coots paddle in the shallows
their black beaks dipping into the duckweed.
Pairs of mallard ducks swim in unison trailing silver wakes.

A golden eagle shadow-hunting above the marsh
perturbs the serenity, stilling the calls of small birds.
Gloved hands curled into warm pockets
and breath puffed out in opaque clouds,
I let the silent refuge hold me.

SUMMER DAYS

Summer days begin in stillness
like the long breath before birthday candles are blown out.
A halo of mist hangs above the mountains
and I throw off twisted sweaty sheets.

Shimmering in rainbows at the edge of the sprinklers,
heat as thick as Maria's enchilada sauce,
envelops the yard and slows my steps
as I shift water from dry spot to dry spot.

After noon, the air is dipped in caramel taffy
and I swelter with leaden limbs
waiting for the hesitant sun to drop
sticky and oozing toward the western horizon.

The long day subsides into pearly night.
As columns of warm air rise from the lawn
I step out into the soft evening
and inhale the perfume of moonlight on sunflowers.

Summer's Last Pleasure

A blackberry—
ripened in the heaviness of a sultry day.
Picked: lavish and bursting.
Sweet and sharp on my tongue.

Warmed by the August sun.
Coaxed by the season,
to bring forth sugar.

One last summer pleasure.

A WALKING MEDITATION

Wrapped like Tibetan monks
in wool scarves and hats,
bundled against the sea wind
we trudge island hills.

Big Leaf Maples drop their giant leaves.
One by one they crash, piercing the silence.
Swirling like thoughts, they settle into
deep piles that crackle around our ankles.

We walk on, eyes focused
on the randomly strewn road
contemplating the intercession of leaves
the deliberate next step.

SALMON GAME

Dulled skinned and red mouthed,
battered fins and tails rose
above the low summer water
as the final run of summer salmon
struggled against the current.

Laughing and splashing, we
hefted the rusty gaff hook
and pulled in fish after fish.
A contest to see who could
snare the biggest carcass.
Soft-fleshed mouths gasped their last
on the muddy bank at our feet.

We played the salmon game
never considering, as we wrestled
the nearly lifeless corpses ashore,
that the fish we snagged would float back
downstream with the first fall rain.
Their bodies and those of their
offspring rotting side by side
in toxic gravel nests.

Like Pearls on my Tongue

Twilight seeps through a
canopy of cedar, fir, and pine.
Rain patters on trails wrapped
in mufflers of red and orange maple leaves.

Near the track, leaves of salal and
huckleberry shed a layer of summer dust.
Ruins of fern and skunk cabbage
collapse into slimy heaps.

I follow the sodden path
until it reaches earth-water and sky-water
foaming over mossy rocks and
coming to rest in pools dotted
with concentric circles of rain.

I tilt my head and newly mingled water
drips from the lacquered tips of fir needles
and falls like gleaming pearls
onto the roughness of my tongue.

Hunting Season

Today I saw the little buck.
The one who sharpened
his horns on my forsythia.

He comes down the hill
to eat what is left of the garden.
One hop over the wall

and he steps beneath
the pine tree that shades the
north corner.

Hidden between the blackberries
and the tomato cages, he
bends so low that from my

window seat all I can see
are the tips of his horns
as he browses on juicy leaves.

The paradox of wild and tame
awakens feelings in me
that have been long buried.

He knows it is dangerous here.
Hunting season has started,
yet he stays, nibbling leaves.

Turning his antlered head,
he looks toward the
house and bounds away.

The voyeur caught
longing for wildness
from a safe haven.

WINTER WRITES

I rise in the darkness of a winter day,
drink a cup of peppermint tea,
and breathe in pungent steam,
as the sun pokes its delicate corona
above the hoary fields.

I am the flannel goddess of dawn
the polyester priestess of birdseed.
I open bins of sunflower and millet
and measure out the right mix
for the finches, sparrows, jays, and doves,
inviting them to a ceremony of food.

Inside, I take off vest, gloves, hat,
and blow on my icy fingers.
I sit at my computer and begin to type.
My fingers move to the rhythms of take offs and landings,
the whirr of wings providing accompaniment
to the melody of my winter writes.

MIDWINTER: SMITH ROCKS

This afternoon no hawks fly,
no ducks float on the swollen river
as a flock of climbers, bright shirts gleaming,
scrabble across the rocky landscape.

Calling to one another from precarious perches,
like flightless raptors,
they anchor to shadowed cracks. Their words
overlap and disappear among the crevices.

Tethered to ancient stone, they listen
as the cacophony of their voices
curls above the roiling brown water
and rises on the sharp cutting wind.

Ascending the jagged wall,
they curl stiff fingers like talons
around coiled rainbows of rope
to grasp the edge of knowing.

THE MCKENZIE RIVER SLOUGH

runs high in winter.
Mud covers the banks and
silt-filled water rises with each new rain.
Bare alder trees crowd the swampy verges,
tenacious roots keeping them upright.

Mist catches in the dormant branches
and thickets of blackberry brambles.
Succulent drops splash from lichened limbs,
dimpling the pliant bog with juicy craters.

In daylight gloom, I walk the newly formed bank.
Mud sucks at my feet, a long drawn-out kiss.
A heron rises from the gloom
and spreads its prehistoric wings.
Worlds outside the mist dissolve—

I lean against a mossy trunk, hold my breath, and wait.

WINTER SHEEP

Sheep in bulky blankets
of greasy waterproof wool
wander on slender black legs,
gnawing their way through
the waterless pastures of winter,
puffing warm breath into
cold air, clouds as round
as their thickset bodies.

Apples, the last of the season,
shine like puckered garnets on
turn-of-the-century trees.
In winter vestments
I swish against the parched
weeds and grass,
the sun warm on my face,
my feet cold in the shadows.

I touch the
knobby, woolly back of one sheep
and then another.
I burrow my fingers into the heavy
fleece and bring them back,
soft, lanolined, and musky
with the smell of winter sheep.

IN SEARCH OF WHALES

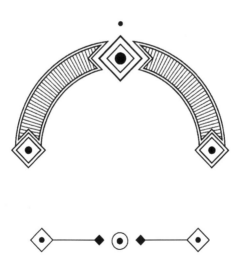

In Search of Whales

On the sandy borderland,
I brace my feet against
the incoming tide
and spend the day in search of whales.

Maybe whales are only myth,
the white dream of Ahab.
A glimpse of fin, a slap of tail
broad backs slide beneath the wave.

Across the expanse of desire,
the leviathan hides itself
from a child's shadow play
the adult need to capture time.

The tide washes my tracks away
but I persist, take a stand
on the point of tangency
and walk the wrack line of imagination.

BEACH HAIR

The nebulous breath of the sea transforms my hair
from domestic curl to alien force.
Frizzy tresses fly around my face in erotic
streaks of blond and gray.

Shaking the dripping fringe, I dance
along the waves in a skirt of foam,
pale green seahorses bobbing among
the strands of my kelp forest hair.

My toes touch the freezing water
and I celebrate the primal child
and aging woman that come alive
beneath a tousled head of beach hair.

INTO THE EBB

On the coast, clumps of houses
anchor to jagged headlands
clinging like strings of mussels
to knotted knuckles of land.

Written in furrowed script
across the fragile sand
their salty stories
spread a foaming narration

of love and loss
that swirls in tidal pools
like transparent mystery
until it vanishes into the ebb.

Her Place

Everything is just the way she left it.
Geraniums blossom along the walk,
red petals enlivening the weathered gray walls.
A secret garden lies beneath the kitchen window.
Rhododendrons that capture raindrops on their leaves,
daffodils in bud, the first nasturtiums unfurling.

Each spring, she flung the windows wide
and opened the cottage to summer.
Reveling in the warmth on her face,
the breeze that rippled her silver hair
the weak rays of the sun
driving out the smell of sea damp.

He never comes anymore.
The place is tender, a bruise touched too often.
Yet he can't discard the memories. Shared weekends,
seals on the beach, the cry of gulls,
sunny days, and intimate nights.
To him, this will always be her place.

DROWNED DREAMS

When the light slants
at the perfect angle
and you shade your eyes
you can see the watery image
of a man's sunken dream.

Beneath the wake of motorboats
the tip of a spar all that
is visible.
All that remains real
in the above wave world

He plotted silently
to sail away
from greed, grasping,
and the need for more.
He craved

the freedom of the sea
riding the crest of adventure
wind in his face
salt rime on his lips and
not having to come
back on Monday.

An Extra Hour

We spent our extra hour today
watching a storm roll in off the Pacific.
Breakers tossed giant logs
and threw globs of foam
like ambrosia at our feet.

Savoring the weak sun
that graces this northern isle,
white caps glowing beneath a too-blue sky.
We take deep breaths of air
charged with an overabundance of oxygen.

At the height of the storm,
we search the waves for the humps of whales,
sway, hypnotized among the drift
and revel in the extravagance
of time running backwards.

BAPTISM

Imagine, standing on the back of gray whale
your bare toes clasped in rubbery flesh,
arms flung outward in the wind.

A whoosh erupts from giant lungs
and sends a geyser of warm,
salty, used water skyward.

And there you stand,
drenched, reborn, joyous,
in the oily breath of whale.

FRIDAY NIGHT POETRY READING

Crisp new books
teeter precariously
on a rickety card table
amid a collage of women
who sidle between narrow aisles
in the makeshift theater.

Balancing paper plates of cheese
and plastic glasses of wine
they nod and smile greetings
while searching for
the perfect copy
to be signed.

In plush seats, they relax
draw deep breaths
and watch the reticent poet
approach the podium,
in a swirl of black silk
and turquoise.

Humbled by her offering,
they receive
her sacrificial meal
in communal silence
and contemplate the infinite
defined by her words.

WHAT THICKETS HIDE

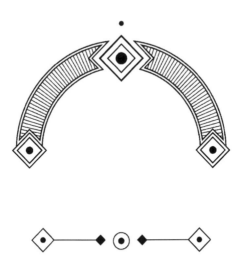

THE LAST DAY OF NOVEMBER

Under a slate gray sky,
through grass thick with dew and deer sign
I swing my legs, letting winter muscles find their rhythm,

On the bank above the road, a juniper spreads its branched
fingers.
A barberry bush only a few days ago covered in orange
is stripped by migrating robins.

Thickets of sumac behind an empty office
hide a cache of broken wine bottles.
Those who dumped the mess, in church this Sunday
repenting.

An old man comes toward me
his voice rubs on itself like rusty wire as he rasps a
greeting.
I am silenced by the fog and nod in return.

A small group of houses behind the fire station are shrouded
in mist.
Every other house is for sale.
"Three bedroom, two bath, conventional financing!"

This close to the solstice, the sun is a fantasy.
Sweat trickles beneath my flannel shirt and I tuck
my tingling fingers inside the cuffs.

A perfect leaf stuck to each shoe, and
arms flapping like an awkward quail,
I run for home.

THE SECRET LANGUAGE

My grandfather thought the language
that tied him to the "old country"
was the vernacular of oppression.

Our youthful, unsuspecting tongues
accepted the offered English eagerly
with no thought of traditional syllables.

Yet I longed to be inside the mystery of that language,
thinking that some secret truth was hidden
between the unintelligible lines.

A few phrases were all I learned,
"How are you?" "I am fine!"
and a short children's song about sleighing.

Translucent as smoke, my culture
vanished over two generations
leaving echoes in the back of my throat.

Womb of Womanhood

Women with sagging breasts
and the slack-muscles stomachs
of child bearing—
sink into the scalding water
of the on-sen.

The heat and steam enter them
as once they allowed only a
lover to touch them.
Surrounding their bodies
in warm mineral wetness
they drift off into a heat haze.

Like babies, they
float in a womb of womanhood
cleansing away reality.
Poising on the edge of consciousness
they drift; and then—
rising as from a dream

they dress, while billows of the past
trail behind them over the tile floor.

HOLY LIES

Our mothers, the keepers of female lore,
hid the mysteries of blood in cryptic texts,
and could not reveal the enigma of our gender.
The appearance of bright blood
smeared our girlish limbs with virgin gore.
Enduring this restive entrance into womanhood,
we reluctantly embraced the viscous knowledge
kept from us by silence and holy lies.

ORIGAMI

"My mother is a poem I'll never be able to write,
though everything I write is a poem to my mother."
— *Sharon Doubiago*

Mountain fold, valley fold,
colored paper becomes
tulips, kimonos, shirts, and daisies.

My fingers caress the paper
folding laughter, tears,
happiness and heartbreak into each design.

Onto a white, pink, or blue card
I glue them, then
add a note of reassurance and sign my name.

I imagine her turning the key,
tearing open the envelope,
tears glistening because I am far away.

So, I fold Japanese paper
into helmets, fans, and fish,
pursuing the ritual journey of daughterhood
reshaping my love.

My Father's Clothes

My father's clothes were
his prized possessions.
He wore them like armor
and folded them with precision.

She acted as if the clothes and
shoes could swallow her.
Dumped his dresser
on the floor and filled bags for the mission.

Buzzing with hysterical
intent, she would blurt out,
"He wasn't even sick!"
"What size shoes do you wear?"
"These are brand new!"

She stuffed his life
into bundles and bags,
but no matter how hard she tried
she couldn't give away her grief.

Bone Hunter

In the time before names,
her fingers became gravedigger's tools.

The earth a sepulcher, a vault
to be unsealed with trowel and brush.

Through a spinal opening of bone,
moonlight reflected on the pale iris of her eye.

Her dreams shrouded in ancient lore
encased in mud, unbreakable.

Daffodils

The trailers are old in Gervais.
They hunker on flat tires among frowsy beds of daffodils.
In a narrow park, steel cactus sprout in patches of narcissus

as sagging houses slide sideways over strips of yellow
and vinyl reindeer stare out the dirty window of the
     general store
at a tangle of daffodils across the street.

At the edge of town, a one-shrub graveyard
rambles through a unkempt field of daffodils,
the swaying golden headstones of spring.

THE SEARCH FOR PERFECT

Toward the coast, we drive
through sporadic rain.
Juicy drops splatter our windshield
leaving behind soggy pastures
and occasional rainbows.

Passing through the unfamiliar landscape,
we search for the perfect oak.
One that stands alone
symmetrically flawless, solemn, and ageless.

Its gnarled trunk and splayed limbs
frame the misty horizon,
sinuous branches dividing the sky
into smaller and smaller pieces of gray,

but there is no perfect oak and
never a good spot to stop;
myriad defects take away
the tree's glorious completeness.

In muddy silence,
these flawed oaks have earned their lives
and we too are scarred, no longer symmetrical beings
choosing to give up the search for perfect,
accepting the beauty of imperfection.

FORBIDDEN FRUIT

At the end of the gravel road
we come to a padlocked gate.
"No Trespassing" signs
tilt crazily on every fence post.

Standing close on tiptoe,
we peek over the gate and look into
a venerable orchard,
branches nearly breaking with fruit.

The gate kept us out,
made us feel intruders, but
like Adam and Eve
gave us a glimpse of Eden.

GLOBAL IMPLICATIONS

The sculptured bones of his shaved head
fit together as seamlessly as
the continents before the drift.
Ebony hide throbs with the
pulse of ancient blood.
The inhabited regions
of his skull slide skeletal plates
along the faults beneath his skin.
Jaws flex, revealing a mortal seam.
With reckless disregard for global implications
he turns his head and stares at me.
Imploring me to interpret the sacred story
that hides behind his smoky eyes.

FORTUNE COOKIE

In the crowded food court,
she sits alone eating take-out Chinese.

Finishing her lunch, she closes the
plastic lid and breaks open

the fortune cookie.
Without reading the fortune,

she folds it and puts it in her shirt pocket
saving the future for later.

NEW ARRIVAL

"Language is the only homeland."
—*Czeslaw Milosz*

He stands half dazed in front of the local quik-stop,
an open bag of Cheetos
tucked like treasure in the crook of his arm,
drinking in gulps from a plastic bottle,
washing away the past.

An immigrant of hope,
he leans on a post, a nylon duffel
of clothes at his feet,
turns and stares west
toward the hazy future.

He shifts his weight
from one foot to the other
looks at the passing cars
his life suspended between two languages.
Waiting....

FENCES

Miguel and Maria
live down the street
in a different country.
Their house is filled with
brown-eyed children and
the soft vowels of Spanish.

Two fences away,
our home is quiet.
We live an interior life
empty of children
but full of memories.

In their yard,
chickens cluck and
the smell of roasting goat
blankets the neighborhood
with the fragrance of chili.

Our yard is still,
but for the buzzing of bees
among the lavender.
Butterflies sip nectar amid
the scent of sweet peas.

With small bags of cilantro,
baby gifts, and a few Spanish phrases,
we reach out to overcome the barriers
that divide us.
Believing that fences
don't define our humanity.

FRONTERA

Small groups of people stumble
from the stairs of the *Fronteras Del Norte* bus
onto the parking lot of Martina's Market.

Standing beneath a "Welcome to Madras" sign,
they shiver in clusters of three or four
smoking, drinking, eating burritos.

Skinny young men and dark haired mothers,
arrive in this desert town carrying
the hopes of Sonora, the dreams of Guadalajara.

Suitcases and neatly tied cardboard boxes
are heaped around the knees of those
who wait for a cousin, an aunt, a promise.

Sleepy-eyed, some stumble back up the steps
and continue riding to Hood River or Yakima,
their *frontera* extending north as far as need.

MIME

What if your life's work was silence?

Everyone knew your name
but not your voice
your expression, but not your words
emotions expressed, by walking
against a wind that doesn't exist.

THE TASTE OF ROCKS

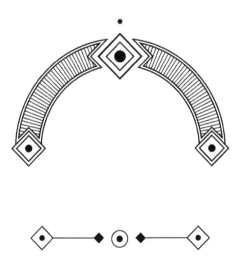

THE TASTE OF ROCKS

Scuffing along a deer trail
through ragged sagebrush
my toe stubs
on a half buried stone.

Once I would have licked
away the dust, rolled the
rock between my teeth
saliva dissolving the grime,
but these days my teeth are fragile.

I put the agate in my pocket,
feel the chill of ancient rock
through the fingers of my glove,
rub the surface in my palm,
until it warms to my touch.

At home, I wash away the dirt
exposing the agate's transparency.
I turn the rock slowly and
touch it with my tongue,
and wonder when I lost the taste for rocks.

TRADITIONS

With drum and flute,
we imitate
the ancient music of stars.
The invisible work of life.

Does a boundary of seas
activate the imagination?
What are the hidden sources that
allow us to glimpse the infinite?

Pulling from memory
and delving into the spiritual,
we keep watch on the space between words,
all the wild unadorned places.

All the prayers that linger in stone.
The eternal presence in moss.

One Point Perspective

Staring down
through a myopic lens
fish-eyed, flattened images
spread across
gelatinous corneas.
Hand tinted in pale
ribbons of morning light,
a glimpse of paradise
from a great height.

Running Away

My cousin says gypsies lived
in the deserted department stores
that line the marble canyons of Portland.

Her stories of thievery and palm reading were
as exotic to me as the bright
silk used to divide the cavernous spaces.

On the summer sidewalk, I gaze upward
clothed in a veneer of requirement,
and raise my hands above my head.

In a gesture of surrender,
with golden handcuffs sliding from my arms.
I embrace gypsy life

packing essentials in a
leather satchel and
running away without baggage.

GIRL WITH AN ATTITUDE

No one sits near her.
She radiates attitude.
Mouth turned down, lips pouting,
arms crossed over an undeveloped chest,
a cup of coffee cooling on the book-strewn table.

Lank-haired and pale complexioned
she looks through me with
a blank, closed stare.
I remember that introspective loner,
the girl who lost herself in books.

I walk on by.
She sits alone
in a bookstore coffee shop just
holding on and holding in
all that should be released.

EPIC AND HAIKU

The world is your home.
At ease in Egyptian desert, Indonesian jungle,
Canadian country lane, or bustling French market,
you embrace the alien, learn foreign tongues,
become familiar with ancient customs,
search the tides of exotic shores.

I am conversant with more intimate landscapes.
A grassy verge of a gravel road,
or rocky shore.
I scan the forest path
focusing on a single otter track,
maple leaf, or a striped limpet shell.

We write separate dialogues for living,
but connect in the intimate conversation of women.
The words: wife, mother, daughter, unite us
as we love, nurture, and create.
Your life the epic, mine the haiku, but
immutably linked by the feminine vernacular.

Elusive Words

I am the mother of pearl
that shines inside an
abalone shell.

The subtle roar of
the sea, secreted in
a curled conch.

A sunflower strong and tall
but always twisting
toward the light.

I am elusive and sly
shimmering like a mirage
just beyond the reach of my own words.

TRAVELING ROSES

In front of a rented house,
sit pots each containing a single rose.
For weeks I have watched,
thinking they would be planted,
but now its fall and the
plants are stripped of their foliage.
Never watered or moved
symbols of impermanence.

Perhaps they've traveled a long way,
a legacy from mother or grandmother,
dug up but never thrown away,
riding in the broken-down trailer,
protected by plastic tubs,
a reminder of better times.

He held the thorny stems with thick gloves
as she dug them in order.
First the Paul Scarlet
that twines along the porch rail
then Peace, a Damask,
Dresden Doll, Fairy Moss, Prosperity
Moonlight, Celestial, Grandmas Lace,
Autumn Delight, and another half dozen
without known names.

All old favorites,
their roots tucked reverently in familiar earth,
ready when the time comes.
The sheriff, sad-eyed, handing over papers,
escorting the family to the truck,
leaving behind two rows of holes.

DELIGHT AND DESIRE

I walk along the poetry
section of the bookstore, running
my fingers along the spines of volumes
filled with the inspiration of varied muses.
I pull a slender book from the shelf,
Why I Rise Early by Mary Oliver.

My heart beats faster, and my breath quickens.
I caress the silky covers that contain her heart,
turn pages inhaling the scent of pine, saltwater, and bracken.
I want to name her discoveries, join her invented dance,
and answer unasked questions.

I balance on the edge of her world,
a woods and shore I have never walked.
Soar on a paper wind, and look down from
a cloud of words into the hurricane
of thoughts that flow from her reality to mine.

I gulp them raw like oysters and lick
them thin, a child with an all day sucker.
Like a scavenging gull, I pick up
a white feather and tuck it between
the slick pages with trembling fingers.

Crossing the line between delight and desire,
I immerse myself in the grammar of her ecology.

THE STING OF THORNS

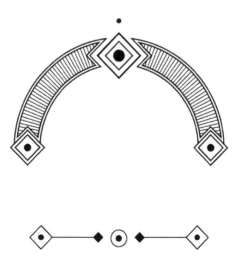

THE STING OF THORNS

Everything has changed.
Home isn't home anymore.
Death and illness have mutated my life
and I don't think about
some of the things that made my childhood special.

My sister urges me, "The blackberries are ripe,
let's go pick some for you
to take home." I hesitate.
The afternoon is hot,
sultry in a way I'm not used to.

I think, *I don't remember blackberries in September.*
But she says, "It's a good year, we had so much rain."
So, plastic bowls beneath our arms, we walk
through the shady maple forest
and out onto a path lined on both sides
with brambles taller than we are.

Clusters of ripe berries droop
just out of reach,
but using clippers doesn't
protect us from the thorns.
Each berry, a juicy treasure
taken forcefully from the briars.

My vulnerable arms
traced with bloody tattoos,
the price of taking home
remembered sweetness.

SHUTTING OUT THE NIGHT

I sit cross-legged in a quiet room
an open book in my lap forgotten,
and stare through the darkening window

while the frail winter day
yields to the heavy march of night.
Shadows lengthen and the distant trees

become silhouettes then disappear and
frozen flowers, broken and naked,
are all that are visible.

The glazed snow glows with its
own light as if sleeping volcanoes
deep underground give it an internal radiance.

Footprints of shadow deer reveal a sodden path,
an opening, a way to see farther
in the darkness of solstice.

I am uneasy on these long nights.
Stilled by snow, winter's songs are frozen,
muted lyrics heard through smothered ears.

I force my eyes back to the page
I realize I have read before,
reach up and lower the shade.

A Winter Portrait

Across the dark of the winter yard,
in a pool of light
I see you bent over your painting.

The room behind you a cavern of darkness,
as rays of light fall along
your face and hand like a Vermeer portrait.

A glow fills in the hollows below your eyes
and defines your familiar face.
Watching you draw, illuminated in the

bluish dimness of twilight,
my throat constricts with the desire to
keep this moment forever.

DANCING WITH GRANDPA

Your work-roughened hand
took my tiny one.

A gentle arm around my waist
swinging my feet off the floor.

Dancing round and round
blonde hair and bald head

close together in polka time.
Stubbled cheek touching soft baby skin.

Tobacco and sweat mingled
with talcum powder.

Grandpa's beating heart.

THE PHYSICS OF TIME

Neck-deep in clouds of
lavender scented bubbles,
I close my eyes and
muse on the physics of time.

The pull of gravity
that widens my hips,
compels my breasts to sag,
thrusts the riparian corridors
of my body earthward.

Scars displayed on
my flaccid belly;
proof that I have conquered
significant mountains.

Weighed down,
heat-weak, dizzy,
I rise from the bath
and rub a worn pink towel
over my changed body.

I need no mirror to show me
the effects of life's passages.
I am a witness to my own demise.
A life lived in the certainty of mortality.

Then you enter the steamy room,
cup my breast and bury
your mouth in my still wet hair,
I smile. As long as you are
here, there is still time.

EARLY MORNING

The silence before
first words are spoken,
so precious and tender.
A new day of possibilities
and you breathing beside me

IF YOU'RE LUCKY

You share the same
favorite star;
you know—the brightest one
in the center of Orion's belt

or sit side by side
barefoot in the sand
watching waves break
on an empty beach

walk through a dusty
marketplace, holding hands,
laughing, eating figs, wrapping
yourself in vermilion silk

And if you're very lucky

you can hold the
wounded half of your soul
in trembling arms
until it can no longer stay.

Then release it
like the whitest dove to soar,
while you, rooted to the earth
stand and watch it go.

A NEW WORLD

The days stretch, long and empty
as her brain collapses in on itself.
Synapses snapping, randomly
mixing memories and metaphors
a chain of scattered dots she can't connect

She deals with the acute agony of blankness
having to learn new customs, new language,
meeting friends over and over again.
An insatiable vague wanting that is never satisfied.

The primal craving for something, anything,
to make sense of her fractured new world.

OLD HANDS

The flesh is disappearing
from the backs of my hands.
Skin creased like paper
folded too many times.

Blue veins stand out
like cloisonné wires
waiting to be filled
with turquoise enamel.

Patterns of blood
cross each other and
divide like braided rivers
toward arthritic digits.

Once, hands like these
held mine, turned
the pages of favorite books,
and taught me to stand alone.

Now, mine are the aging hands,
with tendons drawn tight
as puppet strings
reaching back to the mirage of youth.

BEARING WITNESS

In fractured conversation,
she rambles like a wind-up toy
with a half-broken spring.

Standing rigid, hands clenched
and jaws tight, we try to
communicate.

Blood vessels pulse
their inexorable job
of eradicating her memory.

We scrutinize each word, phrase,
and sentence for recognition
of our own aging.

In her wheelchair,
she sits like a wounded gladiator
dueling with the future.

Is this our duty? To witness
the blood sport of dying,
the decline, the slide.

She hangs on, trying to
make sure she still exists,
not recognizing herself.

We squirm inside
waiting for the final,
the mutual release.

MORNING, MARCH 19

Alone in a strange house,
everything is quiet
except for the rumbling furnace.
Marooned in silence, I search,
but even the dog has disappeared

Across town in the hospital
my mother is dying.
Her last breaths tear from her chest,
and all I can think about
is that I would rather be at home with you.

I don't need to see this dying.
I have died by bits the last two months,
my heart torn, but not broken.
Unshed tears are locked behind my eyes,
and my head hurts from holding them back.

Light spreads across the valley floor
but I feel closed in,
no broad vistas of desert or mountains
make it hard to breathe.
Soon I'll be the oldest in my family.

I want to feel joy again.
I long to dig my fingers into crumbly soil,
hold your healing body to my breast,
forget the pain
and start this day again.

MOWING

Around the field, in ever tightening circles,
I mow the heads of a thousand dying dandelions.

Their drying stems slip beneath my blade.
Downy globes shatter, revealing the
exquisite lightness of death.

Circles of pristine grass emerge behind me,
the path that we all must crawl, walk, or dance along.

Reaching the thinly drawn line between life and death,
I wonder, is it better to know what waits
or to be surprised, as the dandelions
they meet the whirring blade?

NEVER FORGET

It is funny the things you want
when your parent dies.

Over the years, my father
had turned cypress knees
into gnome like men.

I always tried to imagine
where he got these gnarled
pieces of wood. They were so light,
it was as if all the life had been dried out.

But he carved life back into them,
working with small tools, and imagination
he formed them into his own image.

While he was carving,
I would compliment him,
say how special they were,
but he never offered me one.

I now possess
five of his cypress men.
They stand like a silent Greek chorus
on my windowsill. All his sadness, bitterness,
and disappointment carved into their
faces. Their mouths frozen
in permanent O's of disapproval.

I keep them because I don't want to
forget his failings.
I keep them because I know that once,
long ago, he loved me.

CATCHING SHINERS

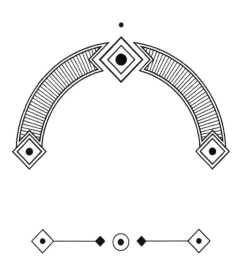

Catching Shiners

Along the winding path,
our shoes scuffed up coarse yellow sand.
The sun so bright,
we squinted our pale eyes
at water glittering
like a million broken mirrors.

With a long handled dipper
and tin pail in his hand,
Dad waded in, fearless,
jeans rolled to his knees.
Leaning into the current,
he scooped up shiners

and poured them
like a wriggling silver chain.
We thrust our fingers
into the slippery, swimming mass,
and sleek bodies slithered
through our caress like memory.

OWNING MY PAST

I am Native American.
My grandmother's family
roamed the forests and swamps of the south.
On bare, calloused feet
they walked single file
silently through leaves
slippery with southern rain.
Steam rising from swampy hillocks
gave their bronze skin a spiritual glow.
Living an inherited life,
handing down a legacy of trust and self-sufficiency.

I am many generations American.
Descendant of hill people who
farmed the Missouri soil.
Clinging tight to hardscrabble farms,
tanned, stringy bodies, working
corn patch and watermelon field.
Sitting on porches askew with decay,
smoking, singing, and telling stories,
living a day-to-day simple existence.
Love of the musky sweet soil,
their generous, reverent bequest.

I am second generation American.
Granddaughter of immigrants,
lured by their vision of freedom,
chased from home by war and poverty.
Passing through Ellis Island's welcoming, oppressive gate.
wrapping Slavic tongues around a foreign language

struggling against the prejudice of newness.
The stink of coal and lumber
heavy in the secondhand clothes they wore.
Hard labor deforming backs and heavy-fingered hands
Courageously embracing untried ways and customs,
imbuing me with patriotic zeal.

I am a child of intermingled blood,
A blended mutt of a person
Who spreads wide, an open net of
ancient and modern roots
unearthing my heart, owning my past.

Sidewalk Revelation

On the sidewalk,
near a new fire hydrant
a footprint.
The brave testament of a passerby
leaving an impression.

The wet cement an invitation to immortality.
A quick glance around
the street fortuitously empty,
the tennis-shoed foot pressed down firmly,
the print distinct and final.

That print stared up at me.
"I'm here to stay!" it seemed to say.
I wished that it were my foot emblazoned there.
That anonymous step
attaining what I strive for.

SEED OF THE OLD COUNTRY

I am the gentle one, the quiet one,
sired by the wind of longing
that blows off the Caucasus.

The fruit of poverty,
carried by the sea to an imagined world.
I was my grandfather's dream.

The child that would speak a foreign tongue,
feel the sun of freedom, grow in the meadow
of choice, flourish in the mountains of love.

Planted in fertile soil and
raised in a landscape of beginnings,
I was his mortal vision of spring.

THE SINGER WITHIN

I sang as a child,
all the bright songs of childhood.
At school, I sang in the chorus.
I loved the sound of my voice,
alone and blended with others.
I was a singer.

Gradually, I gave up singing,
but inside my heart, the songs remained
reminders of the days when
I could shout out the words.

Now, I sing my words onto the blank page
revealing myself.
Someday soon I'll sing again.
Words will jump from the page
and fly from my lips
to fill the air with newly formed song,
the strong, lilting, melody of my reality.

MY LIMITED VOCABULARY

I wanted to say:
>   I wore an Egyptian crown
>   of lapis and turquoise
>   but the words wouldn't come.

I wanted to tell:
>   I danced like a dervish
>   all swirling color and flashing swords
>   but the syllables wouldn't align.

I wanted to declare:
>   I would rise like Venus
>   hiding secrets in cupped ivory hands
>   but my thesaurus failed me.

I wanted to write:
>   my fractured history, but could only
>   relate it in a revisionist dialect
>   dictated by my limited vocabulary.

SOME NIGHTS AFTER YOGA

I bounce through the door
sparkling
with renewed energy
lightness
in my step.

Other nights, I slip from
the car
holding
the stillness
of the practice inside me.

An hour of not speaking
renews my spirit.
The muted sounds
of conscious breath
permit me to sigh out the world.

Silence is my teacher.
Its secret peace
inhabits the creases of my pain
and the being
I was meant to be.

TOGETHER AGAIN

In a crowded pew we sit,
my arm through yours
our thighs touching.

From speakers along the aisle
come the strains of
"Amazing Grace" and
I feel that grace.

I try not to think
that I could be the widow,
the one left behind.

My stomach churns,
and tears gather behind my eyes
but I am reassured
as I stroke your arm.

You are still alive
and we carry on
not quite the same,
but together again.

THE REALITY OF LOSS

We page through dusty picture albums and
I ask about this person or that.
"Who is that brunette girl at my birthday party?"
She shrugs her shoulders and turns her face away.

My mother is forgetting my childhood.

We look at more faded images.
I work hard to keep her attention
Who? When? Where? I almost sob but
she is ambiguous, vague.

I get no answers.

I want to know things that
happened before I could remember,
but I want all this too late.
My mother's failing memory forces me

to accept the reality of loss.

The Language of Death

My best friend calls and
I tell her I have lost my mom
but that isn't true.
I know exactly where she is,
her ashes in a box on a shelf at the funeral home.

I say she passed away, passed on,
is taking the final journey,
has gone beyond the veil, is going home,
crossing the river, heading to the promised land.

Inadequate words,
the human need to put the unknowable into words.
Now she knows the ultimate truth or lie
of what is beyond death
and I am left to wrestle with the language.

THURSDAY THE BAND PLAYS AT MOE'S

The homely holy woman
comes rushing in from the rain,
slings her coat on the back of a chair,
tosses her mousy brown hair,
and orders a bowl of clam chowder.

Born of foam and salt,
baptized by ocean brine
she wipes rain from her glasses,
drinks deeply from a mug of tea,
searches the room for friends.

When the band begins to play,
she listens intently,
becomes one with the music,
sings along, and dances her chair
around the table.

I imagine the girl that she was—
the wallflower, ridiculed,
standing on the sidelines,
her armpits wet with desire,
she would never apologize.

While the band plays at Moe's,
and coastal winds rattle the windows,
she invites us to share the
communion of music,
the sacrament of shared rhythm.

SHRINES

My grandfather's inkwell,
a small silk doll,
and a red bucket filled with multicolored pens.

Dried lavender in a pale blue vase,
poetry books in jumbled rows,
words piled like salt cairns holding the tide.

Among tattered scraps of wisdom,
fragments of prayers, the past folded
into long white pages, I seek my inheritance.

WE SIT OPPOSITE

We squat at a distance from tribal fires
eavesdropping on sacred stories,
the backs of our kinsmen turned away.

We are the listeners.
We sit opposite.

Shadow companions, we benevolent spies
hoard bits of intimate conversation,
weaving stolen words into asymmetrical verse.

We are the poets.
We stand separate.

ACKNOWLEDGMENTS

Thanks to the editors of the following journals in which these poems, sometimes in different versions, first appeared.

These Mountains that Separate Us, "Natural History"
Windfall, "Lady's Slippers and Lambs' Tongues
Shadow Poetry, "Gold Stars"
Tapestry, "The Sentinels"
Honoring Our Rivers, "Refuge"
Shadow Ink, "Summer's Last Pleasure"
Tigers Eye, "Salmon Game"
Windfall, "Like Pearls on My Tongue"
Long Story Short, "Winter Writes"
Mesilla Valley Press, "Midwinter: Smith Rocks"
Windfall, "The McKenzie River Slough"
Windfall, "Winter Sheep"
Tigers Eye, "In Search of Whales"
My Kitchen Table, "Her Place"
Avocet, "An Extra Hour"
Tigers Eye, "Baptism"
Calyx, "Womb of Womanhood"
Shadow Poetry, "Holy Lies"
Tigers Eye, "Bone Hunter"
Bathtub Gin, "Daffodils"
Long Story Short, "Forbidden Fruit"
Anthology, "Global Implications"
Windfall, "Frontera"
Mesilla Valley Press, "The Taste of Rocks"
Tigers Eye, "One Point Perspective"
Beginnings, "Girl with an Attitude"
My Kitchen Table, "Epic and Haiku"
Mesilla Valley Press, "Delight and Desire"
Love After Seventy, "The Physics of Time"
Tapestry, "If You're Lucky"

Tigers Eye, "Never Forget"
Long Story Short, "Catching Shiners"
Cascade Reader, "Owning My Past"
Late Bloomers, "Sidewalk Revelation"
Windfall, "Thursday the Band Plays at Moe's"
Shadow Poetry, "Shrines"
Speakeasy, "We Sit Opposite"

ABOUT THE AUTHOR

MARALEE GERKE lives and writes in Madras, Oregon. She is an avid reader and gardener. She describes herself as "a work in progress."

Her poems have been published in Calyx, Exit Thirteen, Moonset, Bathtub Gin, Anthology, Nerve Cowboy, Avocet, and Tigers Eye. She has published two books of poems and has had poetry and prose accepted in several anthologies. Her work can be seen online at Shadow Poetry, Long Story Short, and Moontown Café.

She recently recorded four poems for the Oregon Poetic Voices Project. They can be heard at oregonpoeticvoices.org. One of her poems was chosen for a special broadside project done in 2012 at the Penland School of Crafts. Her poem, "Natural History," was included in a serial poem with eighteen other Oregon poets. Through this project, she participated in a series of readings in Portland, Eugene, and Pendleton, Oregon, in 2013.